God's Inheritance in You!

You Are the Object of God's Desire!

Rudi Louw

Copyright © 2013 Rudi Louw Publishing

All rights reserved solely by the author. No part of this book may be reproduced in any form *without the permission of the author.*

Scripture quotations are taken from the RSV®, *Revised Standard Version*, Copyright © 1983 by Thomas Nelson, Inc.

Some Scripture quotations were taken from the NKJV®, *New King James Version*, Copyright © 1983 by Thomas Nelson, Inc.

All Scripture quotations not taken from the RSV or NKJV are from the *Mirror Bible,* Copyright © 2012 by Francois du Toit, or are a literal translation of the Scriptures.

The Holy Scriptures are just that, HOLY.

Statements enclosed in brackets were inserted into Scripture quotations to add emphasis or to clarify the meaning of what is being said in those scriptures. The integrity of God's Word to Man was not compromised in any way. Due care and diligence were cautiously exercised to keep the Word of Truth intact.

For example, the apostle Paul said in his second letter to Timothy in Chapter Three, Verse Sixteen that, *"All Scripture is given by inspiration of God* (literally God breathed)*, and is profitable for doctrine, for reproof, for correction, for instruction **in righteousness."*** (NKJV)

Table of Contents

The Marvel of the Holy Bible 5
Acknowledgment 11
Foreword 13
1. *We Are Called Into God's Own Rest!* 19
2. *God's Chosen Portion!* 23
3. *Our Origin in God!* 27
4. *The Only Appropriate Response!* ...31
5. *Love's Total Rest!* 35
6. *Appreciation is the Key!* 39
7. *Blessed!* 45
8. *God Chose Us & Called Us in Christ!* 49
9. *Father, We Give You Thanks!* 55
10. *The Son of His Love!* 59
11. *Eden* 65
12. *Appreciation = Faith's Power!* 73
13. *Children of Wrath!* 81
14. *Propitiation* 89
15. *God's Eternal Purpose* 97

16. *God's Faith, Not Our Presumption!* *103*

17. *Feedback!* *111*

18. *The Apple of His Eye!* *119*

About the Author *129*

The Marvel of the Holy Bible

1. Uninterrupted Theme and Inspired Thought

It took *1,500 years* to compile the Holy Bible, involving *more than 40 different authors*. Yet the theme and inspired thought of Scripture, continues *uninterrupted* from author to author, from beginning till end.

2. Absence of Mythical Stories

Compare philosophies and theories about creation in the Middle East, Europe, Asia, Africa, and Latin America and you'll find mythical scenarios: gods feuding and cutting up other gods to form the heavens and the earth, etc.

In ancient Greek mythology, Atlas carries the earth on his shoulders. In India, Hindus believe eight elephants carry the earth on their backs.

But in contrast, Job, the oldest book in the Holy Bible, declares that, *"God suspends the earth 'on nothing."(Job 26:7)*

This was said thousands of years before Isaac Newton discovered the invisible laws of gravity that delicately balance every planet and sun in its individual circuit.

In sharp contrast to every other ancient attempt to give a creation account, *the Holy Bible pictures the creation of the earth in a very scientific manner.*

For example: In Genesis Chapter One, the continents are lifted from the seas, then vegetation is formed and later animal life, all reproducing *'according to its own kind',* **thus recognizing the fixed genetic laws.** In addition, we have the bringing forth of man and woman, *all done by God in a dignified and proper manner, without mythological adornments.*

The balance or remainder of the Holy Bible follows suit.

The narratives are **true historical documents**, *faithfully reflecting society and culture* **as history and archaeology would discover them thousands of years later. Not only is the Holy Bible historically accurate, it is also reliable when it deals with scientifically proven subjects.**

It was never intended to be a textbook on history, science, mathematics, or medicine. *However, when its writers touch on these subjects,* **they often state facts that scientific advancement would not reveal, or** *even consider, until thousands of years later.*

While many have doubted the accuracy of the Holy Bible, time and continued research have consistently demonstrated that the Word of God is better informed than its critics.

3. Durability

Of all the ancient works of substantial size, *only the Holy Bible survives intact, against all odds and expectations.*

Compared with other ancient writings, the Holy Bible has more manuscripts as evidence to support it than any ten pieces of classical literature combined!

For example, the plays of William Shakespeare were written about four hundred years ago, after the invention of the printing press. Many of his original writings have been lost, and words are missing in numerous sections. In contrast, *the Holy Bible's uncanny preservation has weathered thousands of years of wars, contradictions, persecutions, fires and invasions.*

Through the centuries Jewish scribes have preserved the Holy Bible's Old Covenant text, ***such as no other manuscripts have ever been preserved. They kept track of every letter, syllable, word and paragraph,*** *preserving the text continuously from generation to generation. Special groups of men within their culture were appointed and trained.* **It was their sole duty to preserve and transmit these documents, <u>with perfect accuracy and fidelity</u>.**

Who ever bothered to count the letters, syllables, or words of Plato, Aristotle, or Seneca for that matter?

As to the New Testament, the actual number of preserved manuscripts is so great that it becomes overwhelming. ***There are more than 5,680 Greek manuscripts, more than 10,000 Latin Vulgate manuscripts, and at least 9,300 other versions. Further still, there exists an additional 25,000 manuscript copies of portions of the New Testament. Each one of these are in extremely close agreement with the others.*** **No other document of antiquity even begins to approach such numbers.**

The closest in comparison is Homer's Iliad, with only 643 manuscripts. The first complete work of Homer only dates back to the 13th century.

4. Unmatched Accuracy in Predictive Foretelling

The Holy Bible is unmatched in accuracy in predictive foretelling. No other ancient

work succeeds in this, or even begins to attempt this.

Other books, such as the Koran, the Book of Mormon, and parts of the Veda claim divine inspiration; *but none of these books contain predictive foretelling.*

This one undeniable fact we know for certain: *While microscopic scrutiny would show up the imperfections, blemishes, and defects of any work of Man, <u>it magnifies the beauties and perfection of God</u>. Just as every flower displays in accurate detail the reflection and perfection of beauty, <u>so does the Word of Truth when it is scrutinized</u>.*

Historian Philip Schaff wrote:

"Without money and weapons, Jesus the Christ conquered more millions, than Alexander, Caesar, Mohammad, and Napoleon. Without science and learning, He (Jesus the Christ) shed more light on things human and divine than all philosophers and scholars combined. Without the eloquence of schools, He (Jesus the Christ) spoke such words of life as was never spoken before or since and produced effects which lie beyond the reach of orator or poet. Without writing a single line, He (Jesus the Christ) set more pens in motion and furnished themes for more sermons, orations, discussions, learned volumes, works of art, and songs of praise ***than the whole army of great men of***

ancient and modern times combined." (*The Person of Christ*, p33. 1913)

Today, there are literally billions of Bibles in more than 2,000 languages.

Isn't it about time you find out what it really has to say?

Hey listen, the Holy Bible is all about Jesus, the Messiah, the Christ…

…and everything about Jesus Christ is really about YOU!!

Study Tips:

Read 2 Corinthians 5:14, 16, 18, 19, and 21.

In the light of these Scriptures, it should be obvious that if you want to study the Holy Bible, *you should study it in the light of Mankind's redemption!*

Feed daily on **redemption realities** found in the book of Acts, in Romans Chapters 1 through 8, and in Ephesians, Colossians, and Galatians, in 1 Peter Chapter 1, 2 Peter Chapter 1, James Chapter 1, and in 1 and 2 Corinthians.

Acknowledgment

I want to acknowledge and thank one of my mentors in the faith, Francois du Toit, for blessing and impacting my life with revelation knowledge.

I borrowed the portion on *"The Marvel of the Holy Bible"* from his website: http://www.MirrorWord.net/, as students so often feel they have a right to do with things that come from teachers they respect. Just as Galatians 6:6 says, *"Let him who is taught the Word **share in all good things** with him who teaches."*

A special thank you goes to Vanessa Mills Cappucci for first preaching this message way back in 1987 and impacting my heart with these truths!

To all our other dear friends and family, for all the love and support, and to Chase Aderhold and all those who helped me with this project:

THANK YOU!

Also, especially to my wife, Carmen;

For keeping me real by being my companion in life and partner in ministry,

I love and appreciate you so very much!

Foreword

Thank you for taking the time to read this book.

Let me start off by saying that *I am totally addicted to my Daddy's love for me.*

I am in love with Jesus Christ, *and that is enough for me!*

The love of God is so much more than a doctrine, a philosophy, or a theory. It is so much more and goes so much deeper than knowledge; it way surpasses knowledge. **We are talking heart language here.**

Thus, I write *to impact people's hearts,* to make them see the mysteries that have been hidden in Father God's heart, concerning Christ Jesus, and actually *concerning THEM,* so as to arrest their conscience with it, *that I may introduce them to their original design and to their true selves,* **and present them to themselves perfect in Christ Jesus,** *and set them apart unto Him **in love**,* as a chaste virgin.

We are involved with the biggest romance of the ages. Therefore this book cannot be read as you would a novel: *casually.* It is not a cleverly devised little myth or fable. **It contains revelation into some things, and thus *truth* you may or may not have considered before.**

It is the very TRUTH of God, ultimate TRUTH, and therefore has direct bearing upon YOUR life. **The Word and the Spirit are my witnesses** *to the REALITY of these things!*

Be like the people of Berea the apostle Paul ministered to in Acts 17:11. Open yourself up to study the revelation contained in this book, **to discover for yourself the REALITY of these things**.

Be forewarned! Do not become guilty of the sins of the Pharisees, **or you too will miss out on THE DEPTH OF FULFILLMENT God Himself, who is LOVE, wants to give you**.

Jesus said of the Pharisees and Sadducees that they strain out every little gnat BUT swallow whole camels. What He meant by that is that *some people seem to have it all together when it comes to doctrine and they love to argue.* **It makes them feel important, but it is nothing other than EMPTY religious and intellectual pride.** *They know the Scriptures in and out, and YET they are still so IGNORANT about* **REAL TRUTH that is only found in LOVE;** *They are always arguing over the use of every little jot and tittle and over the meaning and interpretation of* **every word of Scripture,** *but they are still so ignorant and indifferent* **towards the things that REALLY MATTER!**

The exact thing they accuse everyone else of doing though, the precise thing they judge everyone else for, *they are actually doing themselves.* That is **they often downright misinterpret and twist what is being said, *making a big deal of insignificant things while obscuring or weakening God's real truth: the truth of His LOVE*.** *They are always majoring on minors* **<u>because they do not understand the heart of God</u>** *and therefore they constantly miss the whole point of the message*.

Paul himself said it so beautifully,

"...the letter kills but **the Spirit BRINGS LIFE**;"
- 2 Corinthians 3:6

"...<u>knowledge puffs up</u>, but **LOVE EDIFIES**."
- 1 Corinthians 8:1

I say again: *Allow yourself to get caught up in the revelation I am about to share. Open yourself up to study the insight contained in this book, not only with a desire to gain knowledge, but also with anticipation* **to hear from Father God yourself; to encounter Him through His Word, and to embrace truth, in order to know and believe the LOVE God has for <u>YOU</u>** *and get so caught up in it* **that you too may receive from Him LOVES' impartation of LIFE.**

The message contained in the gospel and revealed in this book also, is indeed the very voice and call of LOVE Himself to every human *being on the face of this earth. If you do take heed to it, it is custom designed and guaranteed **to forever alter and enrich your life!***

"Therefore I do not cease
making mention of you
in my prayers

that the God
of our Lord Jesus Christ,
the Father of Glory,
may give you
the Spirit of wisdom
and revelation
in the knowledge of Him,

the eyes of your understanding
being enlightened,

that you might know

what the hope of His calling is,
and what
the riches
of the glory
of <u>His inheritance</u>
in the saints are."

"I pray
<u>that you might grasp</u>
how precious you are to God
as His possession
and as His inheritance."
- Ephesians 1:15-18

Chapter 1

We Are Called Into God's Own Rest!

If God did not express His love in a tangible way by causing His love to take on flesh and blood, *we would still be in a pitiful state, and totally ignorant!* But God **demonstrated His own love towards us** by causing His Son to take on flesh and blood. In Jesus, **God's love for us** took on flesh and blood! We are here on earth *as the product of **that love.***

What a glorious origin to have!

We originated in His love!

Let's begin in Hebrews 4:1,

*"Therefore, since the promise remains __of entering His rest__, let us fear **lest any of you seem to have come short of it**."*

There have been many things attached to the rest of God. But if we truly want to discover **how to actually enter into the rest of God**, then I believe *we must first discover **how **__He__** himself entered into __His__ own rest.***

It says in Hebrews 4:11, *"Let us add diligence **that we may enter into __the rest of God__**."*

In other words, **God has a rest.** He is talking about *entering into **God's own rest!***

We see in the Scriptures that creation and redemption *correlates:* **Creation is a type or picture of redemption!** *Creation is the shadow in the physical realm, while redemption is **the substance** in the spiritual realm!*

To understand **on what basis God rests His case (on what basis God rests)** *concerning redemption in Christ Jesus,* **we must first see** *on what basis God **rested** concerning creation.*

As a matter of practicality in our own lives, *we will only rest, according to the measure of the revelation in our hearts of **why God is at rest concerning us.***

You see, we must see **God's persuasion** *concerning our rest, before we will be persuaded that we can rest concerning our own lives!*

Ephesians 2:10 says that, *"**We are God's workmanship** created in Christ Jesus."*

Now Hebrews 4:3 says that,

*"**God's works were finished** from the foundation of the world!"*

On what basis is it possible **that God's works were finished** *from the foundation* of the world?

That means, _even before creation itself?_

God's works were finished *before creation itself!*

On what basis is it possible **that God's works were finished** *even before creation itself?*

We find our answer in Proverbs 8.

Chapter 2

God's Chosen Portion!

Proverbs 8:22-25 speaks of **wisdom personified** in the person of Christ!

*"**The Lord possessed Me at the beginning** of His way, before His works of old (**even before creation**). **I have been established from everlasting**, from the beginning, before there was ever an earth. When there were no depths **I was brought forth**, when there were no fountains abounding with water. Before the mountains were settled, before the hills, **I was brought forth.**"*

You see, that which has been established **from everlasting** (from eternity past), that which has been established in eternity itself, in other words, *in the very heart of God*, I am talking about ***that love*** *that God possessed* ***at His core*** *from the very beginning,* ***that love was and is*** *His wisdom; His very blueprint, His mold from which He created everything.*

I want you to picture it with me: God was so full of joy, He was so filled with *the abundance of His own love in His inner being* **that Christ was formed in His bosom.**

Ha... ha... ha... Isn't that just wonderful to discover!

You see, He could not *but* give utterance *to what He enjoyed* as His own, and so, from within the Father the Son was brought forth; Christ was brought forth.

Christ is the very core of God, *the substance of the bosom of the Father, and such an exact representation, such an exact match of the Father Himself, and of what the Father desired, that* **He found His full delight in Him!**

He is the apple of His eye, *and occupies the place of preeminence;* *offspring of the Father,* ***the first Son, begotten only of God!***

God's desire, what God purposed in His heart from the beginning, *was to **enjoy** fellowship **in a love relationship, and the Son (Christ) was the fulfillment of every aspect of that!***

Thus, from having **full satisfaction** in the Son (in Christ), *God decided to create nothing else; nothing that would not have the same features as Christ. All God's works would intimately relate to Christ!* **All God's works would only be *an outflow of Christ*** *and not a creation of anything new.*

Creation itself was thus actually *only an overflow of what God enjoyed in the Son (in Christ). It was an outflow of Christ, an outflow of the "LOGOS",* and not a creation out of nothing.

This is why the Greek text in Colossians 1:16 says that,

*"**In Him** all things were created"*

And then it goes on to say that *"...all things were created, **through Him**, and, **for Him**"*

The apostle John put it this way,

"In the beginning was the 'LOGOS' (the Word, the Logic of God; the very thoughts and expression; the utterance of God) *...and the 'LOGOS' was with God ...the 'LOGOS' was 'PROS' face to face with, or **equal** and **intimate** with God;"*

"...and the 'LOGOS' was God (the *'LOGOS'* was the very essence, the very core of God. It was the exact substance of God. The *'LOGOS'* was all of God)..."

The word, *'LOGOS'* is where we get our English words *'logic'* and *'thought'* from.

The word, *'LOGOS'* however *implies more than just a thought. It also implies **the expression or bringing forth of that thought in its entirety.***

Thus, the word, *'LOGOS'* includes the motive behind the thought, and the complete thought itself, thus the reasoning out and the development of that thought, and finally, the expression and communication of the thought.

And so *God's thoughts were destined to go beyond just a silent plan within Him.*

Everything that **was made visible** in creation *already existed in the invisible Christ!*

Thus, visible creation **was the proof _of the success_ of the original blueprint!**

Ha... ha... ha... WOW!

This is the reason why Proverbs 8:30-31 says,

"Then I (Christ) *was beside Him* (The Father) *as a master craftsman; and **I was daily His delight,** rejoicing always before Him, rejoicing in His inhabited world* (in Planet Earth and its inhabitants) **and my delight was with the sons of men.***"*

This is also why Acts 15:18 says,

"Known to God from eternity (or enjoyed by God from all eternity) *are **all** His works."*

God intimately knows His works *from eternity,* because He has determined that no work of creation would be anything else **other than _an expression of Christ_ Himself; an expression of that which gives Him the most pleasure, that which He enjoys most!**

Therefore the whole of creation finds its essential features in Christ! That is exactly how it was possible that God's works were finished, *before the foundation of the world.*

Chapter 3

Our Origin in God!

So let us now discover in Genesis *how God **entered into His rest** concerning his works.*

In Genesis 1 we read how God created the heavens and the earth.

As God's creation plan unfolded (Genesis 1:3, 10, 12, 17, 21 & 25), we read,

"…and God saw that it was good;"

"…and God saw that it was good;"

"…and God saw that it was good"

That word *"good"* means that *everything that God beheld after He had created it* **had the features of Christ. It touched the pleasure of His heart! It found favor in the sight of the Beholder!**

Now I want you to notice here in verse 26 that when God began the creation of Man, *in creating Man He could speak to no other substance than Himself.* And so He spoke to Himself saying, *"Let **Us** 'AWSAW'…"*

*"Let us **bring forth** Man…"*

He speaks to Himself, *because He is the substance that Man is made from!*

*"Let **us** make ('AWSAW' – **bring forth**) Man, in **Our** image; **Our** likeness."*

He brings Man forth *from His own substance, from the 'LOGOS',* **from Christ Himself.** *And thus **He defines Man** with a definition so broad that we could never find its boundaries.*

Man is an eternal being!

If you can define God (His image, His likeness), *only then will you be able to accurately define Man!*

So it says here in Genesis 1:27,

"So God made Man in His own image…"

Genesis 2:7 gives further insight into what actually happened,

"God formed Man from the dust of the earth and breathed into his nostrils the breath of life."

Notice that *the body* God prepared for Man *is not what defines Man.* **It is the breath that God breathed into Man** *that defines Man!* It is the breath that God breathed into Man that is *the essence of Man!*

Let's imagine the actual event: God forms the body of Man. He then leans over and picks up this lifeless form and begins to speak to the substance from which Man is to be brought forth from – **Himself.**

He says, *"**Us, bring forth Man! Our image! Our likeness!**"*

The very *'LOGOS',* the very thoughts and words He speaks, *are the breath, the very Spirit* that transfers Man *from inside of God,* into this body! In essence, **God reproduces out of Christ and Man becomes a living being!**

We were in Christ before the foundation of the world!

We were *before the world was!*

We became part of creation, *but creation is not our beginning, our origin,* for we are brought forth out of the *'LOGOS',* out of Christ Himself, out of God our Father, out of the Son, out of the Holy Spirit, out of that Holy Trinity, **out of the fullness of the Godhead!**

We were brought forth out of the eternal Spirit of God.

Thus we are eternal beings. We are spirit, we are infinite, without beginning and without end! Every bit as eternal as that Spirit and *'LOGOS'* we came from! Every bit as eternal as Christ Himself!

Hebrews 2:11 says that, *"...both **Jesus Christ and us** ...**are all <u>of One</u>** (we are **from the same Source, from the same Origin** ...**we are <u>of the same Substance</u>** ...**we are all <u>of One</u>**) ...for which reason **He is not ashamed to call us, <u>brethren</u>**!"*

Chapter 4

The Only Appropriate Response!

Let's get back to Genesis 1:27,

"So God made Man in His own image,"

"God made Man; male and female He created them,"

*"…and then God **blessed** them,"*

"…and God said to them, 'Be fruitful and multiply and fill the earth and subdue and have dominion over it."

Verse 31,

*"And God saw everything He had created **and indeed it was very good**."*

Note that each previous time after God created *"God saw that it was good,"* but this time, after God made Man, *"God saw everything **and now indeed it was very good**."*

The word ***"blessed"*** used in verse 28 is the Hebrew word BAWRAK- and as it is used here, maybe not in all other instances, but as it is used here in this instance, it can be defined as ***an act of adoration such as kneeling***

It means that God appreciated them!

He adored them!

It is kind of like someone kneeling and scooping up their own newborn baby to admire him or her.

I know that to the religious mind this might be too much, and it might seem like heresy. But in the light of the fact that *Man was brought forth out of God Himself,* and in light of *God's own declaration* in the statement, *"God saw everything and NOW **indeed it was very good**,"* I am telling you, that the word *"**blessed**"* used in Genesis 1:28 *truly does say that **He fell on His knees because He was overwhelmed in His appreciation and adoration of them; of Mankind, of us!***

He adored us! He appreciated us!

Thus Mankind awoke to the appreciation of God! Man's very first experience was *the overwhelming display of God's love;* God's very favor and adoration!

God is LOVE!

And this love, LOVE himself, could only REST, in an encounter... an encounter with a being of the same kind; of the same likeness as Himself... someone made in His

image... a being with the capacity to love... a person able to respond and resonate and reciprocate the love of God!

Love can only find its rest in love!

Love can only be satisfied by love!

Love desires someone else to love!

God, in His creation of Mankind, desired a being with whom He could share equality; companionship!

He desired a being upon whom He could lavish His love!

God desired a response of the same quality in that being, called Man!

I say again: In God's creation of Mankind, **He** *desired a response of the same quality!*

We were the fulfillment of His very dream for companionship; *someone to lavish His love upon and someone who could love Him back!*

See, Man alone can appreciate and respond to God's love on a level of equality.

The very desire in Man to worship God was birthed by the experience of God's adoration.

To reflect back in love the adoration He gives is the only appropriate response!

In 1 John 4:19, John says, *"We love Him because He first loved us."*

Paul essentially says in Ephesians 1:7 that, God did in redemption, *the exact same thing He did in creation.*

In redemption God lavished His love upon us!

Why would He do this?

God wanted the same results!

God wanted to restore things back to the way they were in the beginning!

Chapter 5

Love's Total Rest!

See, in creation **God could only enter His rest *when He had found a being <u>whom He could appreciate</u>.***

And so, in redemption also, **God could only enter His rest *when He had, in the ultimate expression and conclusion of TRUTH, created a being <u>whom He could wholeheartedly appreciate and adore</u>:***

…**the new Man!**

…**the new creation!**

God's rest in both creation and redemption had found its fulfillment *when He was persuaded, and revealed that persuasion, that Man was the full and perfect expression of that being He had longed for and desired in His heart to fellowship with.*

So when did God enter His rest?

I want you to know that **God already found us in Christ, *way before He ever lost us in Adam!* And thus, *He never left His rest!* In fact, *He is still resting!* God has been at rest from the day He created Man!**

So when did God enter His rest?

When He appreciated the work of His hands!

When He brought Man forth from within Himself He said,

*"Man is **very good** (...supremely enjoyable)"*

All of creation was *good*. It has found *pleasure* in His heart; it has found *favor* in His sight. But when He created Man's body and brought Man forth from within Himself, from within His bosom, from within His heart, He said,

*"Behold it is **very good** (...exceptionally good)."*

In other words **Man is the pinnacle of the creative ability of God!**

Within the limits of Man, *within the being of Man, God found everything that satisfied the desire of His heart!*

Thus, the boundary lines have fallen for <u>Him</u> *in pleasant places!*

Ha... ha... ha...

God discovered in Man everything that He needed *to satisfy His own desire for companionship.* **He discovered in Man** *His soul mate, someone He could share His heart and Spirit with!*

God rested, because He found in Man, *the mirror-reflection of Himself!* He found in Man, *the same kind of love, and the same kind of person as within Himself!*

Man was and is indeed the joy of His desire!

That is why it says,

*"...and God said, '**Behold it is <u>supremely good</u>**.'"*

God could rest, because of that *"**<u>very good</u>**"* quality of the creation of Man.

That word *"rest"* means that I have come to a place where **the reality dawned upon me that <u>I need to add nothing to my life</u>!**

Nothing can be added to my person.

Nothing can be added to the PERSON of who I am in Christ!

I am <u>God's</u> creation!

I am *His workmanship created In Christ!*

I am His offspring!

But not only that, **now, in redemption also, in God's expression of the ultimate truth, I am a new creation in Christ Jesus!**

I am that new creation, *even if my experience does not match up with it!*

See, my experience **is only an outflow of my knowledge, an outflow of who I think I am!**

Even as a Christian, my experience is only an outflow of who I think I am in Christ, *but the truth is, my experience cannot add or take away from who I really am as a person, who I really am, who God says I am, and sees me to be, <u>because truth is defined in God</u>, not in me!* *I cannot vindicate or even challenge what truth is, through my experiences in life, not even if my experience* **seems to be contrary to** *who I am in Christ!*

Indeed, *"Let God be true, and every man's experience be a lie!"* - Romans 3:4

The reality that you need to add nothing to your life is indeed a very strong reality to live in! It means you are living in the consciousness that you experience ultimate satisfaction!

To rest is to live your life *being in a state of absolute peace.* To rest is to *walk conscious of absolute peace, to be in a state of absolute assurance,* to be in *absolute confidence,* to experience *absolute tranquility, and absolute love!*

He entered His rest, because of you being in a state of completeness!

When we discover that as truth, we are set free in the now to enjoy that completeness as our reality! Hallelujah!

Chapter 6

Appreciation is the Key!

So <u>how</u> would *we* enter **the rest of God?**

In the light of what I am sharing with you, *would you agree with me that it is:* **to appreciate <u>as</u> God appreciates?**

So now I start to appreciate my creation. I am God's creation, the offspring of God, my true Father! I start to appreciate my identity in Him. I start to appreciate the new creation within me, *as God alone appreciates me,* **because, through appreciating** *as He does,* **I would certainly enter into the rest He enjoys!**

Appreciation is when I salute the work of another person on my behalf.

Appreciation is to acknowledge God for the good and perfectly complete work, which He did within you, in creation, and which He then also reaffirmed in Christ.

And so, therefore all that I can do in reaction to God's perfect workmanship in Christ Jesus is *to respond in full appreciation.*

Why was God's interest in creation so focused upon Man?

What was God's purpose with Man?

Was He looking for some profit in the works of Man?

If God genuinely sought profit from Man's work, *then He should have created him on the first day, and then together with Him, Man and God could have planned and worked together in creation;* **Man adding his little bit to adjust and improve on God's *perfection!***

If His interest was in the profit He could gain from the works of Man, then He would have created him on the first day, *and then let him work hard!*

The opposite is actually true in that God Himself, by His own initiative and on His own, *took much time to create everything, in tremendous detail and perfection, not for Him so much, but **for Man to enjoy.***

See, we could have made everything, **but God made it for us, so that we would not be disrupted in our rest, always wondering if He is satisfied with His profit margin, and the quality of our work!**

Listen, that leads to religion, not relationship. God wants nothing to do with religion. He is after one thing only: an intimate love-relationship; not religion!

See, Love took much time in His love when He created creation. He took much time in depositing love's wealth into the earth. God could have given us just black and white, *and we would have done well. But no, He went to His ultimate in designing an earth wherein Man would get to know Him in the extravagant display of His abundant love.*

In the garden of Eden God created the perfect circumstances, *and an atmosphere for perfect romance!*

He went to the ultimate of His creative thought when He created the world. He spent much time creating, even though it says, one day, one day, one day.

The Word says that a thousand years is like one day to God!

Ha… ha… ha…

You see, after He completed everything, then God made Man, because the one thing that He desired was that *everything must be completed before the advent of Man, so that Mankind could enjoy the full expression of God's heart in creation.*

God was thorough in creating everything because He had total enjoyment! Utter satisfaction! Complete fulfillment in the expression of His love! But that was not the end reason He was so thorough, He was thorough *because He had total enjoyment, utter satisfaction, and complete fulfillment in mind for Man!*

In all He was doing, He was aiming for Man's heart *in order to awaken love's response!*

Everything had to be completed **before Man arrived** *so that all that Man had to do was* **to get to know Him who is love** and appreciate everything that He had done for him ...*and thus fall in love with Him!*

God went to the extreme and spent a lot of time focusing on the details, **so that your appreciation could be** *a rest and an enjoyment,* **and not a frustration of works to you!**

Listen, it was all done in pure love; **you owe God nothing!**

Everything God has done for you, and given you, *is a gift!*

Life itself is a gift!

You are God's greatest gift to you!

Untangle yourself from works of frustration!

Untangle yourself from anxiety!

Untangle yourself!

Appreciate the gift you are, *and unwrap yourself!*

Discover yourself in Christ Jesus!

You are complete in Christ!

Discover your completeness!

Chapter 7

Blessed!

Genesis 2:1-2,

*"Thus the heavens and the earth and all the host of them were finished, **and on the seventh day God ended His work,** which He had done."*

God entered into His rest, never to exit it again!

*"Then God **blessed** the seventh day."*

God **blessed** all of creation, but the *only day* He **blessed,** was the seventh day.

Why?

He sanctified it! The word sanctified means He **"set it apart."**

God set that time apart as special, and made it a special time of celebration, because of **His rest** from all His works.

God's rest therefore, is a celebration of perfection!

He sanctified the seventh day for Himself and Man, *to enjoy together, and to enjoy each other's love!*

It was a day of celebration, wherein God would discover and explore *His rest.* And thus it became a time, an existence for Man in which to celebrate; **Man would explore and celebrate the perfection of creation, as well as his own perfection in God's eyes, and discover God's rest, and thus enter into his own rest also.**

"...God rested from all His works!"

That word *"rest"* means **He came into a state of tranquility. He ceased from all exertion.** It was not because He finally exhausted His energy and had nothing left to give! His rest was not the rest of frustration, boredom, or slumber, no, **it was a celebration in** *the doing away of exertion,* **but in no ways was it a rest of inactivity!**

It was a celebration, an enjoyment of love in all its creativity and activity! It was the celebration of the birth of Mankind. **It was the celebration of the birth of God's baby, God's dream;** *the fulfillment of His desire!*

All that was left was enjoyment! God enjoying Man, and Man enjoying God! It was a total celebration of life and love, an utter enjoyment, a renewal of being and energy; a discovery of a new unending inspiration and joy!

God's rest was a rest of total satisfaction!

Isn't that precious?!

The first day that Adam and Eve ever lived on the face of this earth was the Sabbath: ***a day of mutual enjoyment, and satisfaction.*** The Sabbath day was sanctified and set apart ***as a momentous time of perpetual celebration and massive enjoyment for both Man and God.*** It was a holy day, ***a day of romance, full of enjoyment and appreciation and adoration-inspired fellowship!***

Even working together, tending to and enjoying the Garden, *added to Adam and Eve's fulfillment and satisfaction, and their appreciation and adoration of God. This only served to further **inspire their fellowship and love relationship with God and one another!***

Isn't that something?

Their work in tending to the garden *only added to their experience of contentment and fulfillment and satisfaction.*

Wow!

How terrific life was in fellowship with God, and still is, for those who discover and enter into His rest with Him!

Chapter 8

God Chose Us & Called Us in Christ!

In looking at the book of Ephesians, we will see that the verse that forms the basis of the whole book is Ephesians 1:4.

This verse captures the most beautiful, amazing truths meant to enrich our faith;, it says,

*"God **chose us**, (or identified us, or united and associated us) **in Christ** before the foundation of the world…"*

"…in love having predestined (pre-designed or planned) *us…"*

*"…according to the **good pleasure** of His will."*

In other words **our identification of who we are did not come *after the Fall*.**

Isn't that good news?!

God initially, and permanently, identified Man in Christ, *even before creation, and this was the cause of everything that followed; the cause of **all of creation!***

It says in Colossians 1:13 that,

*"…the kingdom of God is the kingdom of **the Son of His love.**"*

*"…**in love** having predestined* (pre-designed or planned) *us…"*

John 1:28 says that,

*"…this Son is **in the bosom** of the Father."*

The word *"**bosom**"* speaks of being in, and enjoying, **that *essential* and *eternal* place of *blessedness* with the Father.** It speaks of **being in the intimate presence of the Father.**

This is the place that the Son of God fully *occupies and lives in now, and fully lived in **even before creation.***

See God the Father was *so inspired by the intimacy that He enjoyed with the Son, that He saw in the Son, in Christ, the potential of many brethren.* **He saw Him becoming the master copy of the whole human race!**

He desired to see many sons!

It says in Hebrews 2:10 that,

*"It was **fitting** for Him;"*

*"…**to bring many sons to glory.**"*

And so God created and redeemed Man *through the inspiration that He received from intimacy with Christ, the Son.*

*God's eternal purpose has always been **for Man to enjoy what His Son enjoyed and still enjoys; to delight in that place in the bosom of the Father-** the eternal and essential place of blessedness in absolute union with God!*

And so he says here in Romans 8:28-29,

"...and we know that all things are made to work together for good (even if it didn't start out that way) *for those who love God;"*

*"...to those who are called **according to His purpose.**"*

We have discovered God's purpose for us, *and that is, to dwell in and occupy the same place as His Son occupies and lives in!*

We are called *according to* **His purpose!**

"For whom He foreknew, He also predestined;"

"...to be conformed to the image of His Son,"

A better translation would read,

*"...He pre-**designed** or **planned us** ...or **jointly formed** us in the image of His Son;"*

51

*"...that He might be **the firstborn among many brethren.**"*

I want you to see that **God desires you to dwell in and occupy no other place than that place His Son occupies and lives in!**

With Man's fall *there came a hindrance* in the purpose of God, *but we have discovered that God's purpose is like a bulldozer!*

Ha… ha… ha…

To Mankind it might have seemed like four thousand years or more dealing with the Fall, but to God that time was like a second. He would not rest in His obsession, *in love's obsession,* until He had redeemed us once again; *until He had reconciled us once again.*

Nothing could hinder His eternal purpose for Man!

Man would be the reproduction of that which God experienced in the Son; in Christ.

Man would be the fruit of His Son; the fruit of Christ.

*Nothing could stand in the way of God's purpose **for you and for me. Nothing!***

The whole of creation was inspired by His intimacy with the Son in the Holy Spirit. This is such a precious truth! That is why

God's plans for Man, and His dealings with Mankind are so strong.

The inspiration that God gets through intimacy with the Son, that desire *to include Man in that same intimacy,* has proven to be so eternally determined, so powerful and unquenchable, *that nothing could stop it.*

Not even the combined sin of Man placed on Christ could put out the fire and passion of God's love for Man!

"God is faithful;"

"...<u>who has called us into the fellowship of His Son</u>." - 1 Corinthians 1:9

That word *"called"* speaks of **a summons by royal decree!**

Wow!

That call is so strong that *nothing will be allowed to hinder it.* It is every bit as strong and unrelenting *as God's eternal love!*

Can you sense the strength of the appeal of your Father's heart of love, *for you, and for all the rest of His children, to be reconciled to Him?*

Isn't that awesome?!

Chapter 9

Father, We Give You Thanks!

Colossians 1:12,

"Giving thanks…"

All that Paul could do **when he discovered God's fulfilled purpose** was *to give thanks.*

That is all he could do!

No other action would be more appropriate!

No other response would be right or fitting!

The Greek word for *"thanks"* is the verb of the Greek noun for *grace!*

Giving thanks is a spontaneous outflow of *seeing that grace which was given to you in Christ Jesus.*

"We give thanks** (or appreciation) **to the God and Father of our Lord Jesus Christ, who has blessed us with every spiritual blessing, in Christ Jesus." - Colossians 1:12

We are filled with gratitude!

Remember that song from the 1980's: *Give Thanks With a Grateful Heart?*

It is all that we can do in response to a perfect creation, and a perfect redemption.

No other action would be more relevant!

*That is all God wants us to do: Celebrate His perfection, and be thankful, **and enjoy its reality!** That is all that is left for us to do. Otherwise God would have created us on the first day.*

*All that Adam could do was to appreciate and enjoy the completed creation, **himself included.*** **Adam could not add to anything that God created, *not even to himself!***

You see he could have been created on the first day, and then he could have said,

'Well Lord, let us add to the elephant, and how about changing the lion, and while we are at it, how about changing and adding a few features on myself here or there as well.'

Ha... ha... ha... **No! He could not add to himself; *he could not add to anything.*** **All that he could do, all that was left for him to do, was to enjoy and appreciate; *entering into the rest that God Himself had entered into!***

Do you see how precious and valuable the relationship is in the Spirit between the Father and the Son?

When you understand the relationship and the place of the Son in the heart of the Father, *you will finally understand the place you occupy in Christ, the place you are in, and live in as well!*

Colossians 1:12-16,

"Giving thanks to the Father, **who has qualified us, to be partakers of the inheritance** of the saints, in the light,"

"He has delivered us from the power of darkness (ignorance, confusion, lies and deception), and translated us into the kingdom of **the Son of His love.**"

Isn't that beautiful?

Chapter 10

The Son of His Love!

*"**He** has translated us, into the kingdom of (into the domain of), **the Son** of His love."*

It says, *"...the Son **of His love**."*

He has translated us into the domain of the Son; the domain of sonship. **He has translated us into the domain of His love.** We have been translated into the domain of **love,** to live under that domain and to enjoy that domain; **the domain of love!**

*"**In Him we have redemption!**"*

Hallelujah!

*"In Him (in the Son) **we have redemption** through His blood, **the forgiveness of sins.** (By God's doing!)"*

*"**He (the Son) is the image** of the invisible God, (He is, the Son is, Jesus is) **the First-born** over all creation."*

*"For **by** Him all things were created, that are in heaven and on the earth, visible and invisible;"*

"...whether thrones or dominions or principalities or authorities;"

*"...all things were created **through** Him, and **for** Him."*

*"And He is **before** all things;"*

*"...and in Him **all things <u>consist</u>**."*

This is the precious place that the Son occupies as the apple of God's eye.

*"All things were made **through** Him, **for** Him, and **unto Him**, and in Him all things consist."*

The word *"**consist**"* means that **all things find their essential features in the Son of God.** In other words, **all things that were created** *were inspired by the Father's intimacy with the Son, in the Spirit.*

All things find their essential features in the Son, *and now through His blood, **through that enormous display of His love for us, He has bought us and redeemed us, and freed us to once again find our features and conviction concerning ourselves, in Him, the Son, the authentic and original Son!***

That word *"**features**"* means that **our image, the substance of our being, the substance of our faith, is found in Him, the Son.**

Jesus Christ was brought forth and presented as <u>the very blueprint</u> of all of creation and all of Mankind!

If the blueprint or the prototype is a success ...*then the product must also be a success!*

That is why when the Fall of Man happened, *no one else could prove the design, or prove the success of the design,* **but the Master Copy.**

If God the Father created all of Mankind **through the inspiration of the Son,** *then the Son Himself* **must prove the success of the design of Man.**

That is why **it could only be the Son of God** that took on flesh and blood. **No one else could qualify!** No one else could redeem Man! No one else could prove that God's creation in Man was a success, *except the only begotten* **(the authentic original)** *Son!* - John 1:14

Christ has come to redeem us back to the bosom of the Father!

He has come to redeem us to that place of rest that Adam should have kept walking in!

John 14:1,

"Let not your hearts be troubled, you believe in God, believe also in Me. In My Father's house are many mansions (dwelling places, or abodes. In other words, **there is room in His heart, in His bosom, for you!**);"

"...if it were not so, I would have told you so."

"I go to prepare a place for you ...and if I go and prepare a place for you..."

(He is talking about that place in the bosom of the Father, the same place He occupies and constantly dwells and lives in. In His death, burial, resurrection, and ascension He prepared and made that place of abiding in God available for you and for me!)

He says, *"I go to prepare a place **for you,** and since I am going and preparing that place **for you** ...I will come again ...and receive you to Myself***

*What does He mean by, "...**I will come again**," and by, "...**and receive you to myself**?"*

What He was saying is: *'I will be raised from the dead, **and you with me,** and I will then ascend, **and you with me,** to the place I have always occupied in my Father's bosom, and thus the Father and I **will release** the Holy Spirit; that Spirit of Truth, **to come and abide with you and in you forever.**'*

*"...since I am going and preparing that place for you, **I will come again and receive you to Myself, so that, where I am, there you may be also**,"* says the Master Copy.

*"...**so that, where I am, there you may be also**,"*

I want you to see this clearly.

John says of Jesus in John 1:18,

"No one has seen the Father at any time;"

*"...but the only begotten Son **who is in the bosom of the Father**, He has declared Him."*

He says in John 14:3,

"...I have come to receive you unto Myself, so that, where I am, there you may be also."

Those mansions are not mansions in the sky, but, ***it is a place of dwelling in God. It is a place where I find my absolute satisfaction,*** as well as **a place where God has found His absolute satisfaction!**

I believe that the Sabbath rest can be termed as ***God's unhindered enjoyment of Man and Man's unhindered enjoyment of God!***

Now I want you to see that in the same way as Adam could not add to the creation of God, *you as a new creation* **cannot add to what God created you to be and declared you to be in Christ.**

He says in John 14:3,

*"...I will come to you and I will receive you unto Myself, **that where I am there you may also be.**"*

Clearly, it takes nothing from your side in order to be in that place of blessedness! You are there already! Do you see that?

Ephesians 1:3-4 says that,

"God blessed us with every spiritual blessing, in Christ Jesus;"

"...even before the foundation of the world."

God created you in Christ, and it is God who put you in Christ Jesus and then redeemed you, before you even knew it!

The Scriptures clearly say in Ephesians 1:10 that, *"...when the fullness of time came, God brought everything in heaven and earth back together in Christ; He brought it back into Christ."*

"Of God you are in Christ, and that not of yourselves" - 1 Corinthians 1:30.

You may pray for twenty hours, sing and fast and jump before God, or even go and preach for ten years if you'd like. **But,** *"**Of God are you in Christ!**"* ...**not of yourself are you in Christ!**

He says that, *"I will come and receive you to Myself,* **that where I am there you may be also.**"

Chapter 11

Eden

What do you need to do to enter in and experience that place of blessedness you already occupy in Christ Jesus?

All you need to do is appreciate it! That's all! Simply embrace it in your heart! Allow yourself to fully appreciate its reality and to fully enjoy its reality!

If God entered His rest through the full appreciation of what He created, *then I enter into my rest as a new creation through my full appreciation of what He created me to be in Christ Jesus, through what He did and revealed in the work of redemption!*

I enter into my rest through my full appreciation of Him and the love He manifested to me and still has for me!

I believe it was Adam's *appreciation* of his own creation, and his appreciation of everything that was created for him by God, *as well as his enjoyment of God Himself being made visible in it all* **that made Paradise a paradise.** Without that appreciation and enjoyment, and intimate fellowship with God **not even Paradise itself would be paradise.**

The very word, *"Eden"* is made up of 3, sometimes 4 Hebrew syllables. It is not easy to translate, but as I was reading and meditating on the definition of the term, *"the garden of Eden",* 4 words came up in my spirit: **Spot, Moment, Place, and Presence.**

And it was then that I realized that, no matter where on earth, **wherever Adam was, that *was the exact spot, the moment, the very place, where Adam enjoyed the nearness of God.***

Thus, the whole earth can be described as a garden, and *"garden"* **is the only word that can be used to describe what Adam enjoyed with God:** *life, beauty, peace, fulfillment, fruitfulness, abundance, enjoyment.*

I believe that that is why no one has ever been able to find this *"Garden of Eden!"*

Ha… ha… ha…

Because wherever Adam was that *was the spot, the moment, and the place, where Adam enjoyed the presence of God.*

*The Garden of Eden represents **an intimate relationship with God, through appreciation of Him and His beautiful work in us and in His magnificent creation.***

Adam's appreciation of creation was such a normal response, *in the light of awakening in a perfect atmosphere and creation; a perfect paradise.*

When God created Adam, everything was already finished and completed, *including Adam.* And so, when Adam awoke in creation, *the only thing that was left for him to do* **was the enjoyment and appreciation of everything around him.** Hence Adam found himself in the Garden of Eden; *in Paradise.*

That is the reason why appreciation could not be works to Adam. ***It was a normal response out of perceiving what God has done!***

Creation is a type or shadow to redemption!

In redemption, after the Fall of Man, *God did the same as He did in creation.* **God finished the whole of redemption, before Man could awake in his salvation!**

In Ephesians 2:11-16, we see that God reconciled, redeemed, and restored, the whole world (both Jew and Gentile), ***back into one new Man,*** *through the cross, in the body of Christ Jesus.*

Through the death of Christ, every single individual was freed from the old Man, from that old identity, and made alive together with Christ, literally, legally, as an eternal reality, *so that every single one of us may* *hear God, understand God, and respond to God.*

God simply brought Mankind back to where Adam and Eve were before the Fall, *back to the "Garden of Eden" ...so that, as they hear the Gospel, they can now again* **respond to it with appreciation, as they embrace the truth of the message!**

I have news for you: **Man was not made new and alive at his decision for God!**

Ha... ha... ha... Okay, yes, he was, **but really he was made new and alive, *when he died and was made alive <u>with Christ</u>, at the cross, and in the resurrection.*** – Ephesians 2:5-10.

Every person that responds to God does not have his or her own cross and resurrection!

What I mean is: *When we see the truth of what happened in the work of redemption,* **we are actually only coming into the <u>experience</u> of that reality! But our experience <u>does not make it any more of a reality</u>!** **The truth of our redemption in Christ Jesus' death and resurrection has ALWAYS been true!**

It had been truth *long before we discovered it. But our discovery of it made us rich* ...just like discovering gold in your back yard would make you rich!

But you didn't put it there, *you only discovered it there!*

Ha… ha… ha…

Now isn't that something!

Oh how precious!

Thank you, Father God!

Hebrews 9:25-26 says that, *"**Christ died once and was resurrected once**." And so, you see, **if you were not part of that,** if you don't see yourself **included in that,** then you have missed the point of it completely.*

All of this is confirmed by the fact that, on the Friday of the cross, the Law still emphatically stated that the whole of Mankind was unacceptable to enter into God's presence, **but on the Monday after the resurrection, the invitation came to all Mankind to enter into the presence of God by the new and living way.** (Hebrews 10:19-22)

God fulfilled the Law by cleansing Mankind at the cross, through the offering (through the gift) of the body of Christ, and what is being said through it. Do you see that?! *Otherwise an invitation to enter would not be possible.*

When God's work of redemption was accomplished, right after that, right after the resurrection, *the Gospel came to the whole of*

*Mankind, in order **to awaken them,** unto what was already completed!*

It corresponds to what He said on the cross,

"...it is finished!"

That is also why 1 Corinthians 15:34 says,

*"<u>**AWAKE unto righteousness**</u>, and sin no more..."*

You cannot become <u>it</u> or work for <u>it</u>, all you need to do is awake unto it, *because you <u>are it</u> already!*

All you need to do is embrace it as <u>truth</u>, *and <u>be</u> what you <u>already are</u>!*

Nowhere is there a command to <u>become</u> dead to sin and alive to God.

There is no such command, *because you just have to <u>**RECKON**</u> yourselves <u>as</u>* **(already)** *dead to sin and alive to God in Christ Jesus!* - Romans 6:11-13

In redemption God has finished everything.

You can only **awake to the fact** that you, as a person, *are already complete in Christ,* **and** *you now have to conclude it to be so!*

It's a faith thing, a revelation thing, from start to finish!

Either you see it and embrace it or you don't! Either you awake to the fact that it is so, *and fully appreciate it,* **and reckon yourself included in that work of redemption, or you don't!**

It's that simple!

Entering into salvation doesn't have to be a difficult thing! It's easy! *Just embrace fully, and appreciate fully, your redemption!*

Psalm 17:15,

"As for me I will see your face in righteousness;"

"I shall be satisfied when I awake in your likeness."

When you heard the Gospel, *you awoke* ...and then *saw* that there is nothing left to be done to become the image and likeness of God, **because you are already that, through creation.** *And now it has been confirmed, and restored unto you, in all reality, and in all practicality, in redemption!*

You have indeed been freed *to again see it, appreciate it, enjoy it, and live it!*

God has already restored you back to one new Man at the cross, a new creation; you and Christ united again, joined ...*one in spirit with Him!*

All that is left now is to enjoy it!

Just appreciate fully what you became in Christ at the cross and resurrection.

...And when you do that, when you identify yourself with Christ, and embrace that identity, God's identity of you, revealed in Him, as your true identity, you will receive the indwelling of the Holy Spirit, that Spirit of Truth that will seal you. - Ephesians 1:13

The Holy Spirit, that Spirit of Truth will seal your identity, He will confirm your sonship, and reinforce your relationship with Father God, and He will cement these truths in you!

"He, who is joined to the Lord, is one Spirit with Him." - 1 Corinthians 6:17

I want to repeat this hugely significant truth: If God entered His rest through the full appreciation of what He created, **then I enter into my rest as a new creation,** *through the full appreciation of Him, and of what He created me to be, and also restored me to be, in Christ Jesus, in that work of redemption.*

Chapter 12

Appreciation = Faith's Power!

So often our experience seems to **contradict what the Word says.** *Everything starts giving its opinion against the gospel, and begins to speak to you and say that your experience does not come close to what the Word says; it doesn't match what is declared in the gospel.* Your very experience says the Word cannot be true, *and it tries to challenge* **the integrity of God's Word.**

In a situation like that, **just keep living in the victory, and refuse to become distracted. <u>Just start to appreciate afresh your new nature</u> which God has given you; your renewed and restored nature,** and victory will remain yours!

The truth is: **You have been fully restored to the full expression of your original design and true identity as child of God!** Don't ever waver from that!

"…we have become partakers of that original Divine nature, (His image, His likeness, the love of God,) **through the knowledge of Him!"**

When you get challenged, or you feel under attack, just sit there and *start to meditate* **upon the innocence that has been given to your spirit.** **Start to appreciate afresh and anew that innocence!** *Your spirit-innocence!* **Start to appreciate afresh and anew in your spirit, the purity that is in you, because your original design in creation was** *restored to you in redemption!* **Appreciate the new nature, the Divine nature within you that is your portion, as a result of that innocence,** *and immediately you will find that that* <u>*rest*</u> *becomes a fresh reality and a constant consciousness!*

I am telling you now, if you would just implement this simple practice, you will immediately find that **that <u>rest</u> becomes a fresh reality that dawns on you as the sun dawns!**

Ha... ha... ha... Hallelujah!

Simply appreciate these things, *"...until the morning star rises in your heart..."* - 2 Peter 1:19.

Only then, in that place of fresh appreciation of your redemption, will you start to appreciate more and more, the bosom of your Father, as that place of blessedness that you dwell in without end in Christ Jesus!

In doing this, *it does not say that your circumstances will change immediately,* ***but*** *your inward being will start to overrule the outward tribulation.* - 2 Corinthians 4:16-18.

Day by day the inward Man must be renewed within you, not by looking to the temporary, outward things, *but by looking to Christ as the mirror-reflection of the eternal Spirit that is within you!*

There is a blessedness in *walking in the consciousness of that place of blessedness* **in the bosom of the Father!**

How?

Through the appreciation of the truth that you are there already, and it is He who has brought you there!

God brought us back into the fellowship of the Son, *at the cross.*

In other words, **each one of us, right now, is** ***constantly living in that place where the Son of God is.***

When contradiction comes and your experience does not match up with the Word, just sit there and say,

'Father, I appreciate the fact that Your Son has redeemed me to a place where I cannot add to anything. Right now, I am occupying and living within that special place within Your bosom in Christ Jesus together with Him. I cannot add to anything! I cannot even add anything to my

life, even if I wanted to, because it was all prepared for me two thousand years ago and before the foundation of the earth and now my life is hidden with Christ in God and I am complete in Him. I am going to just enjoy Your fullness, in spite of what I am facing, in spite of what I am going through, in spite of what I am dealing with!'

It was of *His* working that you are what you are; *otherwise if you were physically there, you would have tried to help Jesus do it.*

It is a done deal; it was accomplished by Him in creation and then reaffirmed and reestablished in Him on the cross and in the resurrection!

1 Corinthians 15:10,

"But by the grace of God, I am what I am."

He prepared that place beforehand, *before you or I were even born.*

And what does God desire from you?

Your appreciation! That's all! Simply your full appreciation of these things!

Because, through your appreciation you enter into the reality of it!

See, appreciation and faith are actually exactly the same thing!

Hebrews 4:1-3,

*"Therefore, since the promise remains of entering His rest, let us fear lest any of you seem to have come short of it, for indeed the Gospel was preached to us as well as to them, but the Word they heard <u>did not profit them</u>, **not being mixed with faith** in those who heard it."*

They did not appreciate the calling of God to them through the Gospel.

*"For we who believe **do enter that rest;**"*

"…so I swore in My wrath that they shall not enter My rest, <u>although the works were finished from the foundation of the earth.</u>"

God's eternal purpose was established from the beginning of the earth, so that you would occupy the Son's place in His bosom and live in His bosom, so *that <u>YOU</u> would be embraced eternally in His bosom, in Christ Jesus, and that place in His heart <u>prepared just for you to enjoy</u> was already finished from the foundation of the earth!*

You cannot add to it. *Just become convinced about it, and enjoy it!*

In Hebrews 4:4-7 God urges us *not to harden our hearts,* **but to appreciate the completed work of Christ!**

Let's read it:

"Again He designates a certain day saying to David – Today, after such a long time, as it has been said 'Today, if you hear My voice,' do not harden your hearts."

The calling of God is heard in His voice, His _love-call_ is heard in His _voice_, and His voice and His calling is the Gospel!

Listen; you do not need to call Man through any other means except the Gospel, *because **his heart responds** to the _love-call_ of God.*

He says, *"Do not harden **your hearts!**"*

Hardening of heart and rebellion would be the exact opposite of appreciation.

*"If Joshua had given them rest, He would not afterward have spoken of another day. There remains, therefore, **a rest** for the people of God."*

*"**A rest**" being **your absolute enjoyment of God and His absolute enjoyment of you!**"*

That is the *rest* of God that you enter into!

It is not your rest; **it is the rest of God that becomes your rest, *as you _see_ the reason for His rest concerning you!***

It is tremendously essential **to _see_** that **God finished everything _Himself_.** Because if you do not **_see_ it,** you will try to produce it through your own works.

God is at *rest* because of what you became in Christ Jesus, through the resurrection!

This truth is settled in His heart!

Therefore this truth is now settled in mine!

Start appreciating ***God's initiative*,** because so often, we think it must come from our side, that we must **come into** His presence with boldness, that we must **break through** the veil into the heavenly places, that **we must take action** to approach God, *in the same tenacity as a lion!*

Listen, it is <u>God's work</u> that opened for us the new and living way!

He is the One who drew near to us.

He is the One who drew *you*.

He is the One who called *you in and through the gospel*. Not the other way around!

Our drawing near and our calling upon Him is merely a response to His drawing near to us, to His call of us.

I say again: **Our calling upon Him, our drawing near to Him is merely a response! We are merely responding to His invitation!**

He took the initiative, amen!

Chapter 13

Children of Wrath!

In Romans 5:8 it says,

*"Herein is the love of God **demonstrated**, that Christ died for us, <u>while</u> we were God's enemies."*

He embraced us in His love, <u>while</u> we were sinners. He embraced us in His love, <u>while</u> we were ungodly and hostile towards Him.

He never was our enemy, but we were at enmity with Him!

In Ephesians 2:3 it says that we were children of wrath. **Not children of the wrath of God, as we always misinterpreted it!** We were not children, who were under God's wrath, *but we were **angry children,** and we carried a lot of rage. **We were living our lives in self-destruct mode. We partook of a wrong mindset; a nature of wrath!***

And no, **Man's nature, in and of itself, is not the sin nature.**

The sin nature *is an outside force* that invades us; it comes from evil. It's the devil's nature, not ours. **It may have set up camp inside of Man, *but it was still an alien***

force, foreign to our true design, foreign to what God intended our true nature to be.

Living under the power of darkness, living by the flesh, by the natural alone, living from *a lesser identity, produced in us a nature of vengeance against God. It produced in us a nature that blasphemed the living God!*

The sin nature, through the Fall, *set up government over Man.* **It invaded and subdued the human race and became the law that dominated us:** *The law of sin and death* **- a force that exerted its negative influence upon Man's nature,** *against the true design of that nature!*

Note: If you want to go study more about this for yourself, Paul goes into considerable detail in Romans 5. Read the whole chapter, but start in verses 12-14, and then read again from verse 1, all the way through. Then go and read Romans 7, the whole thing, and then you can also go and study in Romans Chapter 1, from verse 14, all the way through to Chapter 3, verse 20.

Paul explains how the sin nature came into the world, *as a foreign entity* **(Romans 5) and it set up a stronghold inside of Man, ruling over Man,** *negatively influencing us all the time* **(Romans 7),** *polluting and corrupting our nature against the true design of that nature, and making us slaves of sin* **(Romans 1:14 through 3:20).** Then you can also go read *what happened to the sin nature through the death of Jesus,* and **how we are freed from it**. (Romans 5, 6 and 8) I also went into detail about this in two of my books, *'Grace Exceedingly Sufficient'* and *'Resurrection Life Now!'*

But as I was saying, **living by the flesh, by the natural alone, from** *a lesser identification of who we are;* **living trapped under the power of that darkness, under the power of ignorance and spiritual blindness** *produced in our nature vengeance against God.* We **developed** a nature that blasphemed the living God!

But <u>while</u> we were in that self-destruct mode, in that state of anger against God, having been polluted and corrupted as it were, by the influence of the sin nature; <u>while</u> we were in that state, *He embraced us in His love.*

Jesus did not die on that cross **to free God from His wrath, <u>but to free Man from his guilty verdict</u>, and from the power of sin!**

You see God came and spoke to us in a language we could understand and relate to; *the tired old dead-end language of the Law.*

He came and spoke that language, ***but only to introduce a new language; a language of love,*** **a conversation between a Father and His precious son, a Bridegroom and His beloved bride,** *wherein the theme is*

romance, acceptance, and love, instead of law and punishment.

Do you agree that <u>the initiative came from Him</u>?

Start appreciating God's initiative!

Start appreciating God reaching out to you! Because when you start walking in that consciousness, *then it is no longer something that must come from your side, but it is simply appreciating what has already come from His side.*

Ezekiel 16:6-14 is a little graphic in description, *but in passionate love language and clarity* it shows us prophetically the initiative of God.

"And when I passed by you and saw you struggling in your own blood, I said to you in your blood, 'Live!'

Yes, I said to you in your blood, 'Live!'

I made you thrive like a plant in the field; and you grew, matured, **and <u>became exceedingly beautiful</u>.**

Your breasts were formed, your hair grew, **but you were naked and bare.**

When I passed by you again and looked upon you, **indeed it was the time of love;** *and so I spread My wing over you,* **and covered your nakedness.**

*Yes, I swore an oath to you, and entered into a covenant with you, and you became **Mine**, says the Lord God.*

Then I washed you in water; yes, I thoroughly washed off your blood, and I anointed you with oil.

I clothed you in embroidered cloth, and gave you sandals of badger skin;

I clothed you with fine linen, and covered you with silk.

I adorned you with ornaments, put bracelets on your wrists, and a chain on your neck. And I put a jewel on your nose, earrings in your ears, and a beautiful crown on your head.

Thus you were adorned with gold and silver, and your clothing was of fine linen, silk, and embroidered cloth.

You ate pastry of fine flour, honey, and oil.

You were exceedingly beautiful, and succeeded to royalty.

Your fame went out among the nations, because of your beauty, for it was perfect, through My splendor, which I had bestowed on you, says the Lord God."

Now, read it again, but this time, *see how all this happened to YOU in Christ Jesus in the New Testament!*

Oh, how easy it is to love Him, out of such an initiative, out of God first reaching out toward you and lavishing His love upon you! God did all that with you, and to you, in Christ! He did all that for you! *So that you* **simply just need to enjoy Him and enjoy who He's made you to be, and <u>be</u> it, to the full extent!**

Hosea 11:1-8 says,

"When Israel was a child, I loved him; out of Egypt I called him, to be My son.

I taught Ephraim to walk, taking them by their arms, but they did not know it was I who healed them.

I <u>drew them with gentle cords, with bands of love</u>, and I was to them, as those who take the yoke off their neck, and I stooped and fed them.

How can I give you up, oh Ephraim?"

What was the motivation of God's heart, calling Man out of a perverse and crooked generation?

Was it His anger and the Law?

Was it an ultimatum, like a slave-owner?

I mean, Man went and blew everything, and God should just have just judged him and left him. But God says in Hosea 11:9,

"I will not execute fierce anger; I will not destroy Ephraim, for I am God, and not Man, the Holy One in your midst. And I will not come to you with terror."

You see, **God is love.** He is not motivated by the Law, or by anger, for the purpose of enslavement. That is never the motivation of God's heart.

1 John 4:9 says,

*"In this **the love of God** was manifested towards us,"*

"...that God has sent His Son, begotten only of God,"

Note: God sent His uniquely conceived Son – conceived not only in the womb of Mary, but uniquely conceived in the *'LOGOS'* of God; the Preeminent One; the original, authentic thought; the authentic, original blueprint Son; the one and only authentic blueprint Son – the only Messiah, the Christ who alone can qualify to represent Mankind.

God sent Him, *"...**into the world**;"*

*"...**that we might live through Him**."*

*"**In this is love**;"*

"...not that we loved God;"

*"...but that **He loved us**;"*

*"...and He sent His Son **to be a propitiation for our sins.**"*

*"Beloved, if God so loved us, **we ought also to love one another.**"*

Paul writes in another place about this and he says,

*"I do not need to teach you **concerning brotherly love**, <u>because God Himself teaches you</u>."*

God's love initiative, God's love on display towards us, *teaches us concerning brotherly love. It teaches us concerning our true design and our true identity as children of God.*

God's love on display teaches us concerning the Divine nature, *and **we are partakers of that Divine nature*** according to 2 Peter 1:4.

We were made in His image and likeness, *and we were fully redeemed and restored to its fullness, in redemption, in Christ Jesus!*

Chapter 14

Propitiation

I want us to clearly see God's initiative of love in His act of propitiation.

The word propitiation is a term that the Greeks used *when they used to bring their sacrifices to their Greek gods.*

They had many kinds of offerings to their gods as is written in the Vines Expository Dictionary, *"…in order to change the mood of their gods to be favorable towards them."*

So they in all their sacrifices constantly acted in the hope of being able to propitiate their gods. It was a bare glimpse of the prophetic anticipation and strong desire unconsciously inherent within the nations, *in which they in their hearts wished that their gods would become favorable towards them.*

Now it sounds as if *their gods were extremely moody.* **I praise God that our God is not a moody God!** *'…One day I must sneak in, and the next day, He hauls me into His presence, and the day after that, He throws me out again…'* Ha… ha… ha… praise God that is not how our God is! **He is consistent in His love!**

People through the ages may have seen God as a moody old Greek god, *but there is just **no shadow of turning** in the heart of God. No fickleness! Nothing shady! No dark side to have to watch out for!*

Ha... ha... ha... **I do not need to shrink back!**

Hallelujah!

That is why He says that His heart *has no **pleasure*** in those who draw back. It disappoints Him, *because His heart has never ever changed towards Man!*

God desires for us to take initiative, *because He first took the initiative!* He wants you to respond wholeheartedly to what He did wholeheartedly in Christ Jesus, with you, and to you, and for you!

I am possessive over God, only because He was first possessive over me!

Ha… ha… ha… Hallelujah!

Thank you for loving us, God!

Thank you for loving **me**, Papa!

You see, getting back to the Greek concept of propitiation, the Greeks *themselves* had to do these *acts of propitiation*. They had to bring *their own sacrifices*.

The God that we have come to know, the God who revealed Himself in Christ Jesus, *did the act of propitiation Himself, on our behalf.*

He brought His own sacrifice and actually offered Himself, in the form of His uniquely conceived authentic blueprint Son, the One begotten only of God.

God's mood did not need to change, to be favorable towards you! **His mood has always been one of loving-kindness and tender mercy towards you!**

It was your mood that had to be changed!

You see, God's mood, was one of love towards Mankind, even before the sacrifice of His Son. **God's mood was one of being in love with you!**

We were children of wrath and vengeance *against God.* **But now God comes, with His Son, *the Lamb of God.***

The Scriptures say in John 1:29,

"Behold the Lamb of <u>God</u>;"

*"...**that takes away** the sin of the world!"*

Can you just imagine what was going on in the minds of those Jewish people who heard this statement from the lips of the prophet, John the Baptist, concerning the Lamb of God?!

I mean, they were so used to bringing their own little lambs for the last 1400 years, according to the customs their forefathers handed down from generation to generation. Through their sacrifices under the law of Moses they were trying to win God's favor, trying to keep God from getting mad at them, or trying to change His negative heart's attitude towards them ...fearful to even approach Almighty God, and yet now, upon seeing Jesus of Nazareth approaching, John shouts out, *"Behold the Lamb of <u>God</u>!"*

Oh, how God, through John, must have blown their minds! Instead of them bringing their little lambs to try and win God's favor, *now all of a sudden here is God bringing His little Lamb to try and win their favor!*

This Lamb, Jesus Christ, was <u>God's act</u> of propitiation, *God's act of <u>favor towards Man</u>.*

So **in a way,** when those Greeks brought their sacrifices to their gods, ha… ha… ha… **they already had the favor of their gods.** *And yet, here they were trying to win the favor of their gods.*

Ha… ha… ha…

Do you see that? **Because there really is only one God, amen!**

In the New Covenant, **it is <u>God</u>** *who is seeking to win the favor of Man.* **That is why He sent His Lamb.** *He desires to change the mood of the hearts of men.*

This is such a precious reality, and it will enrich your faith and thus your experience in Him *if you make it a point to live in the consciousness of God's initiative over your life!*

In the light of God's initiative, *your walk and relationship with God is not a burden or an obligation,* but it is simply <u>responding</u> **to what He first did!**

Herein is the love of God demonstrated, *in that He first loved you!*

God did not need to be reconciled to you, *you needed to be reconciled to God!*

2 Corinthians 5:18,

"Now all things are of God, who has reconciled us to Himself, through Jesus Christ, and has given us the ministry of reconciliation.

That is then also the heart of our message: God was in Christ, reconciling the world to Himself, you included!"

Why was God in Christ, reconciling us to Himself?

Because He desired godly offspring *in His bringing Man back into a relationship of favor with Himself* – Malachi 2:15.

*"**God was in Christ, reconciling the world to Himself;**"*

*"…**not imputing their trespasses to them;**"*

*"…**and has committed to us** (who see and understand these things) **the word** (the message; the gospel, the good news) **of reconciliation.**"*

*"**Therefore** we are ambassadors for Christ;"*

*"…as though God were **pleading** through us;"*

*"…**we implore you** on Christ's behalf;"*

*"…**be** reconciled to God."*

The word *"**pleading**"* means,

*"…**to seek the favor of.**"*

God was seeking the favor of Man, *desiring a change of mood in the heart of Man towards Him!*

Now on that basis I personally also implore <u>you</u> on Christ's behalf,

*"…**be** reconciled to God!"*

I want this reality of being reconciled to God to so <u>dawn upon you</u>, through the Spirit, that you cannot help but <u>BE</u> reconciled!

Chapter 15

God's Eternal Purpose

In Ephesians 3:8-12 we read about,

*"...**the unsearchable riches of Christ** that is preached to the Gentiles, **to us.**"*

Not the *unknowable*, but the *inexhaustible* riches of Christ!

I want this reality of, the inexhaustible riches of Christ, to so <u>dawn upon you</u> through the Spirit!

This revelation of the love of God and of what has been given and restored to us in Christ **compelled, energized, and motivated Paul in ministry. It was the driving force within him** *"...<u>to make all people see</u> **what the fellowship** (the inclusion, the intimacy) **of the mystery is;**

...which from the beginning of the ages, has been hidden in God, who created all things through Jesus Christ."

"This manifold wisdom of God, is now made known to the church, (to those who see and understand their true identity, and therefore also their identification in Jesus Christ);*"*

"…which is (...this multifaceted, all-inclusive wisdom of God is) *according to the eternal purpose,* **which He accomplished** *in Christ Jesus our Lord."*

What is the manifold, all-inclusive, multifaceted wisdom of God? What is God's eternal purpose? What is the eternal mystery which from the beginning of the ages has been hidden in God? What is that wisdom? What is that mystery?

The mystery that was hidden for Man to discover was that, *for all the ages God longed for and desired mirror-reflection fellowship that would equal and be the same as His fellowship with the Son!*

This *eternal purpose* **(Ephesians 1:3-4)** <u>**was accomplished**</u> **through the incarnation and the work of redemption,** *in Christ Jesus.*

The Fall *disturbed* and *disrupted,* and for all intents and purposes, *canceled out* **the <u>function</u>** *of this purpose in Man.*

But that purpose remained preserved in Christ Jesus as the blueprint!

With redemption, **God**, *through the Blueprint and with His own blood*, **redeemed and rescued the image and likeness of God in Man, in restoring Man to innocence and righteousness again.** **This restoration is what God refers to as the new creation!**

Colossians 1:25-29 says that,

*"...the stewardship of God is <u>the mystery</u> that was hidden for ages and generations, **but now has been revealed** in Christ Jesus."*

*It has been revealed, **as in a mirror!***

What is hidden in us *was reflected in Him!*

The riches of the glory of this mystery, **WITHIN the Gentiles,** *are revealed.*

The mystery revealed **is that *Christ is <u>IN</u> them,***

"...Christ <u>IN YOU</u>, the hope of Glory!"

He fulfills your every hope and expectation!

He reveals the true you!

God has rescued and restored to purity again His image and likeness in Man, *through the incarnation, and through the cross, and through the resurrection!*

Peter put it this way in 1 Peter 1:3 & 4,

"Blessed be the God and Father of our Lord Jesus Christ;"

"...Who according to His great grace and abundant mercy;"

"...has <u>begotten us again</u> to a living hope."

"...He has begotten us again (In other words, **He has given birth to us again**) *through the resurrection of Jesus Christ from the dead,"*

"(He has given birth to us, or awakened us again) *to an inheritance* (to a treasure ...to everything God has for us ...to His whole heart,) *incorruptible and undefiled* (preserved in the eternal bosom of God) *and that does not fade away* (**this eternal purpose and intense love only grows stronger**), *reserved in heaven;* (in the heavenly realm, the unseen spirit realm of spirit reality), ***for you!****"*

God has restored His image and likeness in Man again, through the incarnation, and through the cross and resurrection!

God has made Mankind new in spirit *by purging them in redemption, and thus restoring the image and likeness of Christ in them, which is the image of God Himself!* – Hebrews 1:3

That is why Ephesians 4:22 says,

"Put on (a command in the past tense – in other words, ***let it manifest, be what you are; be, or put on***) *the new Man that was created* (that was brought forth; that was restored to you, in redemption), *according to God* (by God's doing, and according to God's righteousness; according to God's exact image and likeness) *in true righteousness and holiness."*

Another translation says,

"...in righteousness and holiness of the truth."

(Note: **The state of your spirit has been legally restored to righteousness and holiness. Thus, in spirit, you can enjoy the same state as God's Spirit.** *In spirit reality you can now enjoy God's righteousness and holiness; the exact content of His Spirit. In your spirit you can now enjoy the exact content of His Spirit, His love-nature, His image and likeness already within you!*)

I want you to also see what Colossians 3:9-11 has to say:

"Do not lie (do not come in agreement with the lie; do not communicate deception) *to one another,* (rather communicate the truth, **the truth of who God says you are)** *since you have put off the old Man with his deeds, and have put on the new Man,"*

*"...who is renewed **in knowledge*** (This new Man is only renewed **through revelation into this truth.** He is renewed) *according to the exact image of Him who created him,* (according to the exact image of God, who created this new spirit Man; this new spirit reality), *where there is neither Greek nor Jew, circumcised nor uncircumcised, neither barbarian nor Scythian, neither slave nor free,* ***but Christ is all, and in all**."*

Chapter 16

God's Faith, Not Our Presumption!

The result of this successful redemption is stated in Ephesians 3:11 & 12,

*"…according to the eternal purpose **which He accomplished in Christ Jesus our Lord;**"*

*"…**in whom we have boldness and access with confidence through the faith of Him.**"*

I want to read to you a translation that my friend, Francois du Toit wrote, out of the Greek:

"Our union with Him is a result of His faith, not our presumption. He initiated our union; we are not imposing upon the presence or the promises of God! We have obtained an unrestricted and unreserved approach!"

Can I also share this story with you to illustrate the point?

Say I am a girl ...*now I know it's not easy for me to think like a girl, because I am a guy, but I'll give it my best shot.* So say I am a girl, and I genuinely wanted to get to know Jonathan because I have seen him around *and I detected in my spirit that he has a treasure in his personality and in his person, and therefore I need to get to know him.*

So I go to him and tell him, *'Jonathan, please, would you like to come to my house and have some coffee and dessert? There will be cream-cake and biscuits - your favorite.'*

You see, he has my favor, *but I want him to get to know me as well.* I want him to have me as a pleasure in his life, *an enjoyable friend.*

Hey, I'm not talking sexual immorality here okay, so relax Max! Our society has gotten so warped in their thinking; there is hardly any room anymore for genuine friendship that does not regress into sexual perversion. *So get your mind out of the gutter and get that nonsense out of your head, and follow along okay?!*

So I invite him, but he just stubbornly refuses. He just does not want to come, and I am inviting and imploring and pleading with him, *'Man, what are you afraid of? I'm not going to bite you or something ...just come and have coffee with me!'*

And after the third sincere invite, he eventually responds. And he comes to my house, and he is careful, and restrained, and timid in his approach, and he just sits there, staring at the food on the table. And then sheepishly he hesitantly asks, *'May I have one of these biscuits?'*

I mean, come on! I am so excited that he finally responded to my invitation. I feel like leaping up and down, and I am bringing out the cookies and coffee as fast as I can. All I want to do is to get to know him as a person and tap into that wealth, that treasure I know is in his spirit, and yet, there he is, *unintentionally insulting my sincere advances with timidity and hesitation.*

In other words, **hey man, you are not imposing!** And yet he still sits there and says, *'I hope that I am not imposing on your presence.'* **How ridiculous! Doesn't he know that I am totally into him?** *Why give me such a lame response?*

Do you see what I am saying here? Can you see what God is trying to say to you?

Your union with God is a result of His faith, *not our presumption!*

He is the one that took the initiative!

This was not your bright idea, it is His!

Ha... ha... ha... You are not the one breaking down the veil into the heavenly places! **He already did it for you!**

That means it is not you who have to try and draw near to Him! *He is the one drawing you with cords of love!*

He prepared that place for you in His presence, *before you were even born!*

You could not add to that, even if you wanted to!

Do you see what it means **to come boldly?**

Do you see **what God rests in,** what God's rest is?

Ha... ha... ha... Hallelujah!

In God's desire to repossess you, *He already knew what the price would be to repossess you as His own possession!*

God knew that the price of redemption *was His own life!* **The price was the life of Jesus Christ, the authentic blueprint Son,** *begotten only of God!*

He gave that which was most precious to Him *to repossess you!*

He gave His Son!

He gave Himself!

He gave His fullness!

He put His heart on display!

He emptied Himself!

Now He has nothing but *you!*

Do you see that with me?

In giving everything to repossess Mankind, He has nothing as His possession but Mankind!

Even His Son is part of the human race now!

His Son forever joined the human race when He took on flesh and blood!

*And the Father became, "...**the God and Father of our Lord Jesus Christ**"* according to Hebrews 2:14 & 17, and 1 Peter 1:3.

The Son sits in heaven at the moment, as a man, with a physical body!

Paul says in 1 Timothy 2:5 that,

*"...there is one mediator between God and Man, **the man** Christ Jesus;"*

It also says in Hebrews 10:12,

*"But **this man**, (talking about Jesus Christ) after he had offered **one** sacrifice for sins **forever**, he **forever** sat down at the right hand of God."*

There is at this moment, a man, <u>forever seated</u> at the right hand of God, representing you! As long as He is seated there, *you are welcome there!*

And He will remain seated there *forever!*
Ha... ha... ha...

Colossians 1:18 and Romans 8:29 also states emphatically that, *"...Jesus is the firstborn **among many <u>brethren</u>**"*

All this means one thing: **It is a perfect redemption!**

Can you now understand why God is possessive over you?

Do you know what it does to your spirit *when you dwell in the consciousness that <u>God, Mr. Love himself, is possessive over YOU</u>?*

Ha... ha... ha... **Meditate on that! Ponder on it! Think about it!**

I mean, really think about it!

Let me blow your mind, and impact your spirit, and enlarge your heart some more with this:

Zephaniah 3:17,

"The Lord your God is in the midst of you, a Mighty one, a Savior who saves,

He rejoices over you with joy, He rests in silent satisfaction;

...and <u>in His love He remains at rest</u> (He remains at peace; satisfied!);

*...and **He makes no mention of past sins or even recalls them;***

*...**He exalts over you with singing!**"*

If that doesn't give you confidence to start enjoying His presence right now, I don't know what else will!

Appreciate the response of God, *His possessiveness over you!*

All the various religions of the earth are busy with idolatry. *"The heathen worship gods that have eyes that cannot see, and mouths that cannot speak, and hands that cannot handle, and ears that cannot hear."* (Deuteronomy 4:28; Daniel 5:23; Psalm 115:5 & 135:16, and Revelation 9:20).

They all worship idols, *and get no response from that idol.*

But now before you get all self-righteous, so does man-made Christianity. They worship the Law. They worship an idol, an image of God that is not real, an inaccurate image they came up with, through man-made religious customs and traditions. Is it any wonder they don't get a positive response from that idol?! They hardly get any response whatsoever in their religious efforts!

It is because their faith is inaccurate, weak, sick, and anemic, and almost non-existent! All because they do not picture God **for who *He*** *has revealed Himself to be, in His Son, in Jesus Christ!*

No wonder they don't get any response, any positive feedback from Him, or hardly any!

I cannot see any reason why they should continue their relationship with that god; *that idol of religion and Law they worship!*

Why settle for anything less, when an actual genuine relationship and friendship with the real and living God of love and power is available, *and worth so much more than the empty religious rituals and religious do's and don'ts they busy themselves with?!*

I say again: **An actual genuine relationship and friendship with the real and living God of love and power is available,** *and worth so much more* **than empty religious rituals of do's and don'ts!**

God came to set us free from our various religions, *when He revealed the truth about who He really is and who we really are!*

We no longer have to busy ourselves with man-made religion of any kind!

In fact, He came to set us free from our concept of religion altogether, *when He made us alive in our relationship with Him!*

Chapter 17

Feedback!

What is it that inspires your relationship with God?

It isn't your religion, not even if it's the Christian-religion, I can tell you that much!

The only thing that inspires genuine relationship with God **is the feedback you receive from God on a daily basis!**

Now how do you receive feedback?

Through appreciating and meditating upon the Scriptures, *upon the Gospel, upon the truth of the incarnation and of redemption, upon the truth of what God Himself revealed in Jesus Christ; appreciating and meditating upon the love of God <u>for you</u>!*

That is how you receive feedback!

Cultivating such a life of appreciating and communing with God, brings you to a place in your life *to where every action taken even is merely a response in worship of Him; it is merely an outflow of His truth, and reality, and love, engraved in your spirit, by His Spirit.*

I am so glad that we are not busy with a God that we are worshiping *without response*.

Listen, we are not praying towards God! We are not talking to God *without feedback!*

God is a God that has given testimony of Himself and of His love for you, not only in Christ, but also in your spirit, and He Himself is sustaining that witness!

We have a God, who is full of love and emotion over us; *over you!* He exults over you with joy! He is passionately in love with YOU!

When you discover God's possessiveness over you, *you cannot but respond!*

He rests in silent satisfaction *over YOU!*

Psalm 132:3 says,

*"Surely I will not go into the chamber of my house, or go up to the comfort of my bed; I will not give sleep to my eyes, or slumber to my eyelids, **until I find a place for the Lord, a dwelling place for the Mighty God of Jacob.**"*

Verse 7-9,

"Let us go into His tabernacle, let us worship at His footstool;"

"...arise, O Lord, to Your resting place, You and the ark of Your strength!"

"Let Your priests be clothed with righteousness, and let Your saints shout for joy."

Verse 13-14,

"For the Lord has chosen Zion; and He has desired it for His habitation. This is My resting place, forever, I will dwell here, for I have desired it."

That word *"desire"* means **unsatisfied longing, until that longing is satisfied.**

God has chosen Zion, because He so appreciated that which He saw in the human race, that He could enter into His rest.

Love found enough, within the creation of Man, in which it could be satisfied.

All these Scriptures prophetically speak about the work of redemption, *and about **our embracing of that work**. It speaks about **God's faith**, what God saw in Mankind, and what He now anticipates to enjoy in relationship and fellowship with all of us **who have now seen and embraced His love and what He did in Christ Jesus, on our behalf!***

We are the Zion of God! We are the New Jerusalem, *the dwelling-place* of God!

In beholding what God did in His love, *there is an enriching of my faith that takes place! There is a feedback from God that takes place, a constant communication back and forth between the Spirit of God and my spirit!* In beholding the God who is love and the love He has for me *a rich encounter and connection between me and God is established in my spirit!*

Let me tell you, there is such a remarkable difference between true Christianity and religion! They are in stark contrast to each other! **With dead religion** *there is no feedback* **from the individual they worship.** *There is no feedback at all, no inspiration to continue in that relationship!*

Herein lay the difference: In true Christianity, *God has called us to a place that His own Son enjoys, and we have feedback from God!*

Listen, you must get to a point of persuasion of these truths in your own heart! A point where you refuse to live in a relationship with God, *without living in the consciousness of the loving feedback of God that is there in your spirit!*

God has given full testimony of Himself, and of His love, in the spirit of Man, *and He wants you to live daily <u>in the full consciousness of it</u>!*

This sounds like heresy to the religious mind, but David said in Psalm 73:25-26,

"Who have I in heaven but You, O God, and having You (enjoying You,) there is nothing I desire on this earth."

In beholding God, and keeping my eyes upon Jesus, and hearing Love's voice, in the truth of the incarnation and redemption, I get the feedback of 1 John 4:17,

"As He (Christ) *is, so are we* (right now) *in this world.*"

So you can say with boldness, of yourself, what God says of you, *because He has reconciled us to a relationship of equality <u>and mutual encouragement</u>.*

A relationship of equality means that *what must be experienced by the one, must be experienced by the other, otherwise it is not a relationship of equality.*

Do you see what we are involved in? **We are involved with a God who rejoices over us, *a God who is filled with love and passion over us!* We are involved in a love affair with God!**

"How can I give you up, O Ephraim?"

"*My compassion grows warm within Me, over <u>you</u>.*"

*"...**I have created you to be My resting place**, says your God."*

Deuteronomy 32:9,

*"**For the Lord's chosen portion is His people** and Jacob is the place of His inheritance."*

To say something is your chosen portion means that you are saying, *"I desire nothing else; this is my absolute delight; it is my present hope, and my living hope for tomorrow, and even the distant future!"*

God says to you,

"Israel, you are My portion, you are My hope for the future, you are My absolute delight ...in fact, you are My inheritance ...and Jacob, you are the place of My inheritance, the place of My treasure, the place of My fulfillment, the place of My joy and intimate satisfaction, My portion, My companion."

God inherited you! How? **In the death of His Son!**

Ephesians 1:11 tells us in the Greek that,

"In whom (in Christ) **we were made His** (God's) **inheritance**, *having been chosen* (predestined), *from the beginning, for this purpose, in accordance to the purpose or intention of Him* (God), *whose might carries out in everything the purpose of His own will."*

The work of the cross was the initiative of God, *to get Mankind as His chosen portion!*

To secure this purpose and to make sure that it will be an absolute success, He carried it out personally, *as the One who works everything in the universe, according to His will.*

It is absolutely overwhelming to be the focus of *such love, such unquenchable initiative, whereby God is overjoyed to have Mankind as the reward of the success of the incarnation, and of the cross, and of the resurrection!*

Deuteronomy 32:10,

"Jacob, ***you are the place of my inheritance.****"*

"<u>I found you</u> in a desert land, a wasteland, a howling wilderness; ***I encircled you and instructed you.****"*

While we were in a wasteland, **God encircled us.**

Ha... ha... ha...

While we were enemies and hostile in our minds towards God, ***He encircled us, and marked us out, for His own possession.***

I love it!

He then kept us *as the apple of His eye!*

That word *"apple"* speaks of *a being's focus; the focus of that being.*

Chapter 18

The Apple of His Eye!

Psalm 17:8,

"Keep me as the apple of Your eye; hide me under the shadow of your wing."

Zechariah 2:8,

"He who touches you, touches the apple of His eye."

That is why David says;

*"What is Man that You are **mind<u>ful</u>** of him."*

Man has always been *the focus of God!*

We must understand what the purpose *which God treasured within Himself* was: *The thoughts of God throughout the ages, even though they were hidden from Man, were wholly upon Man.* **The thoughts of God *were focused upon Man!* His desire *was focused upon Man!* And everything in the heart of God *was inclined upon Man, and purposed for Man!***

When this happens to you, and revelation knowledge is birthed in you, *and you discover that the mind of God has always been upon you,* **you cannot but become possessed, with the same possession God has been possessed over you with.**

God's mind *is possessed with Mankind!* **He is** *obsessed with Mankind!*

When we realize this, we cannot help but become possessed and obsessed by the thoughts of God over us!

The purpose that God treasured in His heart, throughout the generations, *has now been unveiled to us.*

This is our stewardship, *to unveil and* **demonstrate** *the purpose that God treasured within Himself!*

Our stewardship is to *reveal to Man* **that he** *now is living in,* **and should fully dwell in,** *the place that God's Son is Himself occupying and dwelling in at this moment:* **a place of total possession, one with God, one with the heart of God, one with the thoughts of God, one with God in intimacy, one with God in every way!**

This is the mystery that has been hidden for ages and generations in the Old Testament. This is the mystery hidden: **Christ is in union with Man,** *and thus Man is in union with God.*

The mystery revealed in the New Testament is that *the image and likeness of Christ,* **as**

God's hope of glory, *is again restored in Mankind.*

Of course, because of who God is, and because He desires a genuine relationship based in true freedom, we can choose to ignore this reality if we want, and continue to exist in blindfold mode, *as if it is not the truth about our existence.* I mean, we can even continue to live our lives in full-on self-destruct mode if we want, **but God came in person, He came in Christ to awaken us to the reality that in Him we live, and move, and have our being.** He came to awaken us to reality itself, **and to win our hearts, by His love for us demonstrated so clearly in Jesus Christ;** *and thus to rescue us out of an empty, lonely, self-centered life lived in self-destruct mode!*

Out of the fact that <u>we are God's portion, His inheritance</u>, **we come to the ultimate relationship sponsoring conclusion,** namely, that, **God is our portion! He's our inheritance!**

It is that realization *which fuels our relationship with Him; our fellowship, our intimate connection and oneness of spirit.* – 1 Corinthians 6:17.

"Our life is hid with Christ in God!" – Colossians 3:3.

This is absolutely Biblical *and logical, for in a covenant relationship the two parties* **belong to each other.**

Psalm 16:5,

"You O Lord are the portion of my inheritance and my cup (of satisfaction); *You maintain my lot* (...you are my lot in life, or my allotted portion)."

Psalm 119:57,

"You are **my** *portion, O Lord."*

Jeremiah 10:16 and 51:19,

"The Portion *of Jacob is not like them, for He is the Maker of all things, and Israel is* **the tribe of His inheritance***; the Lord of hosts is His name."*

Lamentations 3:24, *"The Lord is* **my** *portion, says my soul, therefore I hope in Him."*

What an inheritance, *to have God as your portion!*

What a treasure of heart, *to be God's inheritance!*

Ephesians 1:15-18,

"Therefore I also, after I heard of your faith in the Lord Jesus, and your love for all the saints, I do not cease making mention of you in my

prayers, that the God of our Lord Jesus Christ, the Father of Glory, may give you the Spirit of wisdom and revelation, in the knowledge of Him, the eyes of your understanding being enlightened, **that you might know, what is the hope of His calling, and what are the riches of the glory, of <u>His inheritance</u>, in the saints***."*

The whole Ephesians 1 is not speaking *of your inheritance*, but rather *it is speaking of greater things, it is speaking of* **God's inheritance,** *which is* **you!**

It says, *"I pray <u>that you might grasp</u>* **how precious you are to God as His possession and as His inheritance.***"*

That is the beauty of the Gospel!

What happens when I discover these truths? **It fulfills me! He becomes the fulfillment of that unquenchable desire within my heart!** *And also then, when I discover these things,* **I fulfill it! I fulfill that desire within the heart of God!**

In the Living Bible translation he says,

"I want you to realize that God has been made rich, because of you!"

Isaiah 32:17-18,

*"The work (or **the fruit**) of righteousness will be peace, **and the effect** of righteousness, quietness and assurance forever."*

We have nothing to add to our redemption *except to fully appreciate the peace, quietness, and assurance of it forever!*

It gives new meaning to the term: Living happily ever after!

It defines righteousness!

Verse 18,

"My people will <u>dwell</u> in a peaceful habitation, in secure dwellings, and in quiet resting places."

All that you need to do is to enjoy this thrilling and mighty redemption!

I want to encourage you to *start enjoying God!* Start enjoying righteousness. Start enjoying the nature that is within you, it is the nature of God.

In the mirror of Christ, <u>*you see yourself*</u> *as God has always seen you:* Innocent, blameless and pure, without guile!

Wallow yourself in that, and be as happy as a pig in mud!

Ha… ha… ha…

And I am not calling you a pig now okay, so relax Max!

Ha... ha... ha...

Indulge in the liberty of truth revealed! Go ahead wallow in it!

Indulge in the liberty of it! *Because you know that* **you are the image and likeness of the Son,** *in whom* **you find your essential features!**

Enjoy the resting place He has brought you into!

I urge you to get yourself a copy of *"The Mirror Bible"* available online at: www.Amazon.com and several other book sellers.

If you want me or someone who is a part of our team to come to where you are, *anywhere in the world,* and give a talk, or teach you and some of your friends *about the gospel message and these redemption realities,* simply contact us at www.LivingWordIntl.com, or you can always find me on Facebook.

If your life has changed as a result of reading this book, *please write to me and let me know.*

I would love to share your joy, *so that my joy in writing this book may be full!*

"That which was from the beginning,

which we have heard
(with our **spiritual ears**),
which we have seen
(with our spiritual eyes),
which we have looked upon
(beheld, focused our attention upon),
and which our hands have also handled
(which we have also experienced),

concerning the Word of life,

we declare to you,

that you also may have this fellowship with us;

and truly our fellowship is with the Father and with His Son Jesus Christ.

And these things we write to you *that your joy may be full."*
~ 1 John 1:1-4

About the Author

Living Word International as a ministry was started by Rudi & Carmen Louw, because they love to travel and inspire others with the truth of the gospel both locally and internationally.

Rudi was born and raised in the country of South Africa, while Carmen grew up in Cortland, New York.

The Louws function in the ministry of reconciliation (2 Corinthians 5:18-21) and flow strongly with the Holy Spirit and His anointing to teach, preach, prophesy, heal, and whatever is needed to touch people's lives with the reality of God's love and power.

God has given them keen insight into what He has to say to Mankind in the work of redemption, *concerning the revelation of, and restoration of,* **humanity's true identity.**

Therefore, they emphasize THE GOSPEL, IN CHRIST REALITIES, the GRACE of God, the WORD OF RIGHTEOUSNESS, *and all such eternal truths essential to salvation and living the CHRIST-LIFE.*

They have been granted this wisdom and revelation into the knowledge of God by the resurrected Spirit of Jesus Christ, *to establish and strengthen believers in the faith of God, and to activate them in ministering to others.*

Not only are people set free from the poison and bondage of sin, condemnation and all kinds of intimidation, (upheld, strengthened and reinforced by age old religious ideas born out of ignorance), **but many are brought into a closer, more intimate relationship with Father God, as Daddy,** through accurate teaching and the unveiling of the gospel message, prophetic words, healings and miracles.

Rudi & Carmen are closely knitted together with several other effective Christians, church fellowships, and groups of believers who share the same revelation and passion **to impart the truth of the gospel to others, so as to impact and transform the world we live in with the LOVE and POWER of God.**

www.ingramcontent.com/pod-product-compliance
Lightning Source LLC
Chambersburg PA
CBHW071129090426
42736CB00012B/2061